heat heat heat heat heat heat heat heat heat heat heat heat heat heat heat heat heat heat heat heat heat heat heat heat heat heat heat heat heat heat heat heat heat heat heat heat heat heat heat heat heat heat heat heat heat heat heat heat heat heat heat heat heat

heat

The Osbournes
book of quotes

Say what?
special

CONTENDER
BOOKS

A division of the Contender Entertainment Group

First published in 2002 by Contender Books
48 Margaret Street
London W1W 8SE
www.contendergroup.com

This edition published 2002
1 3 5 7 9 10 8 6 4 2

ISBN 1 84357 040 8

Edited by Julie Emery and Julian Linley
Art Director: Mark Taylor
Designer: Darren Heatley
Picture Editor: Mariana Felicio
Compiled by Kevin McCreeth
Enterprise Director for *heat*: Zachary Soreff

Pictures: Bigpictures.com; Imagedirect; LFI; Rex Features; Wenn; Wireimage.com
With special thanks to MTV
Repro by Digicol Link, Kent
Printed and bound in Belgium by Proost NV

Also available:
Say what? Celebrity Sex
Say what? Gareth Gates

heat

The Osbournes
book of quotes

Say what?
special

❝Obviously he's not the typical father who comes home with a briefcase at six and we all have a family dinner. We're not The Partridge Family. **❞**

You can say that again, Sharon

"It's colder than a witch's tit."

Speaking from experience there, are you Ozzy?

Ozzy: "Isn't it terrible the way kids speak these days?"
Kelly: "I learned from you, Daddy."
Ozzy: "Ah, well at least you learned from the best."

Aah, like father like daughter

"Martha Stewart can lick my scrotum. Do I have a scrotum?"

Er no, Sharon. But we're sure Martha Stewart would love it

"No Sharon, you don't need a pet therapist, you just need to get up at 7am and open the fucking door."

Ozzy Osbourne – the new Barbara Woodhouse

"My mother got me my first musical job — I tuned car horns."

That explains a lot, Ozzy

"There was an ad for [*The Osbournes*] on TV… And Aimee was here watching it and she goes, 'This is just disgusting. This is just, like, too much. This is disgraceful. How can you let this go out?'"

The Osbournes' eldest daughter says what a million people out there think

66 Wait till you're 50… How old am I, Sharon? **99**

Ozzy can't quite remember his age

Kelly: "They make you feed a tree before you feed yourself."

Ozzy: "How the fuck do you feed a tree? Put a ham sandwich by it?"

Kelly explains what happens at hippy summer camps. Like, crazy, man

"I hate washing up, I hate cooking. I'm never doing it again."

Time for some home help, Sharon?

Kelly: "It's better than telling Jack to 'go fuck yourself' isn't it?"

Sharon: "No. I think, 'Jack go fuck yourself' is better than, 'Take that dick out of your arse.'"

Kelly: "It's stick Mum, not dick."

Come on Sharon, keep up

" What you have to understand is that me and Jack have been brought up very different from everyone else. **"**

Well Kelly, that's one way of putting it

"There's crucifixes everywhere: we'll never be able to sell it."

Oops. Too late to worry about selling the house now, Sharon

"Jack, you seriously have some anger management control problems."

Kelly seems surprised that Jack's got issues

"There's no way anyone's smoking dope in my house. That's how I started and look at me."

Ozzy says just say no

"Mum, right now Aimee is wearing a thong of mine, so it's been up my crack and now it's up her crack, and I'm not down with that."

Kelly draws the line at thong-sharing with her sister

" Jack gets so squinty when he smokes pot; he looks like Yoko Ono. **"**

Kelly's *so* proud of her brother's impressions

Sharon: "Did he say you've got to keep [your broken leg] elevated?'
Ozzy: "He said I've got to have a naked lady lying on me for the next three weeks."

That's *our* kind of health service

"I hate Christmas. It's just…
Let's sit at a table with your
family and see how long you
can sit there without arguing.
It's the stupidest shit."

Kelly's not one for playing Happy Families

"Please don't drink or take drugs, and if you have sex, wear a condom."

In other words Ozzy, do as I say, not as I do

❝Darling don't get me wrong, I like her. But she don't like me; she's trying to destroy me.**❞**

Ozzy suffers an attack of paranoia over a dog

"Why'd they have to find it in my bum of all places? It's embarrassing. I mean, why couldn't I have had a cute heart-shaped polyp on my vagina?"

Sharon on her cancer

"I'm searching for the man who wrote, 'And they all lived happily ever after.' He's got to be a c***."

Here's hoping Ozzy doesn't find him

"How come none of us can turn the vacuum on?"

See Kelly, it's not easy being an Osbourne

"I mean, it's like, *The National Enquirer* are doing us? What are they going to say? My husband is an alcoholic? Oh, gosh."

Too true, Sharon

"Bubbles! Oh come on Sharon! I'm Ozzy Osbourne, the fucking Prince Of Darkness… Evil! What's fucking evil about a whole load of bubbles?"

Throw in a bouncy castle and we've got ourselves a party, eh Ozzy?

"I wiped my crotch with my hand and chased Kelly trying to wipe it on her. I said to myself, 'There's no way I can let that go in [the TV show]. They'll take my kids away.'"

Sharon's just your average all-American mom

"There is an awful lot of love in our family. I mean, both humans and creatures, you know."

Not sure we do Ozzy. "Hello, is that the RSPCA?"

“Darling, the wicked witch has nothing on me.**”**

Sharon states the obvious

"Why don't you do the right thing, son? It's a man that can apologise; it's a wimp that can't."

Ozzy gives Jack some fatherly advice

"I'm not picking up another turd, I'm a rock star…"

Ozzy ain't gonna clean up after those dogs no more

"They removed more than a foot of my colon, so I'm on a soft-food diet, things like jelly and chicken soup – with no chicken."

Mmm, sounds delicious, Sharon

"Please don't drink or get stoned tonight, because I'm pissed off that I can't."

Just some TV tonight then, kids

"You need a computer to turn on the TV? Why can't we get a normal fucking TV? I press this one button and the shower comes on."

Ozzy's got some seriously dodgy wiring

Ozzy: "What's that in your hair, Kelly?"
Kelly: "It's a flower."
Ozzy: "I thought it was chewing gum."

Ozzy: not entirely down with the kids

"Me and my friend were in the kitchen and my mom comes in, lifts up her shirt and goes, 'Ryan, do you think I'm sexy?' And I was like, 'Oh my God.'"

No wonder Jack's mates are always round

"If you're Ozzy Osbourne's children, man, everybody in town wants to fuck you. And there ain't no coming back from an HIV attack."

Ozzy outlines the perils of unprotected sex, sort of

“All that crap you've got on your lips. How do guys pull chicks with these fucking mouths?**”**
Ozzy: not a big lipstick fan

"We've known about your dope situation for a long time. Don't you think I know what it means when you order a pizza at 12 o'clock at night?"

Ozzy lets Jack know he knows what those funny cigarettes are

"You know why my dog's dysfunctional? Because it's like me. It's angry at you."

Jack agrees with the theory that dogs become like their owners

Sharon: "That son of ours is in bed."
Ozzy: "He's just contemplating his next…"
Sharon: "The only thing he's contemplating is his next wank; whether he's gonna use his left hand or his right."

Well, it's a big decision, Sharon

66 You're the bestest husband and father in the world and we love you. **99**

Sharon in a rare soppy moment

Sharon: "Ozzy doesn't want to, you know, save the rainforest. I mean, he'd like to, but we're not capable of it."

Ozzy: "I'd like to save the forest at the bottom of my garden first – from the dogs who are urinating up the tree."

Charity begins at home, isn't that right, Ozzy?

"I don't mind a little Pomeranian turd, but when that bulldog unloads you've gotta get an earthmover and a fucking gas mask to get in the kitchen. It's like plutonium turds."

Ozzy talks shit, literally

"Mum? You know I'd, like, appreciate if you tell me when you give my dog away."

We didn't even know it was getting married, Jack

❝Jack: You laughed when I got smashed in the face with a baseball bat.
Kelly: Because it was funny!❞
Strike one! A fine example of sisterly love

"Dad. I hate Jack."

Kelly keeps it simple

"He started to take Viagra and we'd wait and wait for it to work, I'd fall asleep and he'd be there with a big boner and I'm fast asleep and he can't wake me up."

Thanks for sharing, Sharon

"It's very hard for me every day to walk into a classroom and be verbally abused. They still can't get over the fact, even though it happened 21 years ago, that dad bit the head off a bat."

Fair point, Kelly

Kelly: "You know why Fred Durst is moving to England? Because nobody hates him there." Sharon: "They soon fucking will."

Just your average mother-daughter conversation

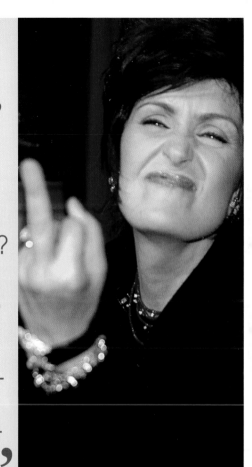

❝Kelly: What happened? You went over there and told them to quiet down? **Sharon:** No… I said, 'Shut the fuck up you middle-aged, something-or-others.'❞

Ah, that's OK then

" My whole life, I wanted to have the dream, the really nice house. Oh, my God, Beverly Hills, how fantastic. You strive to get it and it's back to my childhood of screaming at the neighbours and throwing stuff over the fence. **"**

Sharon's living the American dream. Osbourne-style

"She's my whole world – she's the best lover I've ever had, the best friend I've ever had. She has been my pillar of strength for many years."

Ahhh, we're filling up, Ozzy

"With all these buttons it could give you a blowjob as well as turn on the TV."

Ozzy's still having problems with the remote control for his new TV

" My teeth,
my car, my
vagina, my
business. **"**

OK then, Kelly

❝ I'm begging you Sharon, I'm begging you; no more animals. ❞
Don't make Ozzy bite the head off anything else

"I dropped my Valentino mink stole down the toilet. It smells like an old crotch now it's been down the toilet."

And what were you expecting, Sharon?

"Don't ask me to smell your breath because it'll still make me throw up."

Kelly: always keen to help out her brother

"You should wear your hair like mine."

Ozzy offers hair advice to President Bush

Ozzy: **"What's wrong with me and your mum snogging?"**
Kelly: **"You're too old."**

Age is no barrier, eh Ozzy

66She's my soulmate. If anything did happen to her first, I wouldn't get married again. We're a team.**99**

And what a team, Ozzy

Sharon: I want to hold him down and piss on his head...
Kelly: That's a little bit much, Mum!

Sometimes you have to be a little unorthodox

"This shit [cigarettes] will kill you faster than crack."

Not sure that's strictly accurate, Ozzy

"People keep touching me…
I can't stand it."

Try wearing your mum's mink, Kelly

Sharon: "This is very nice [finding a bottle of Jack Daniel's and a fag]. I'm gonna take a piss in it and put it back."

Kelly: "Don't you dare, Mum."

Sharon: "If you tell him, I'll kill you."

Kelly: "You can't do that, that's not funny. Stop it. That's fucking disgusting."

Sharon: "Well he [Jack] shouldn't have it in his room."

That'll teach him, Sharon

"Cheer up Jack, you miserable fuck."

Gentle persuasion Sharon-style

"Jack seriously, take that huge stick out of your arse and maybe that'll help everyone."

Kelly's such a caring sister

"Why is he seeing that woman with a face like a sack of shit? She looks like a horse's arse."

Ozzy on Prince Charles' lady friend

Sharon: "We found out that one of our 11 truck drivers got into an accident. We found out today…"

Ozzy: "He was stoned?"

Sharon: "No."

Ozzy: "Drunk?"

Sharon: "Getting a blowjob from a hooker while he was driving the truck."

Ozzy: "Oh, that'll do it."

Sharon: "And he was naked."

Well, *he's* not getting a pay rise

"My wife said to Camilla Parker Bowles, 'I think you're fucking great.' My eyeballs nearly flew out of my head. I said, 'Sharon, watch your language.'"

You can't take those Osbournes anywhere

"Just in case you were wondering… you're a shit driver."

We're sure she wasn't, Kelly

" She said that word again! You should have been called Vagina Osbourne. **"**

Don't think Kelly would have liked that much, Sharon

66 The Virgin Mary speaks to me. She says, 'You must go to Tiffany, and on the way, stop at Cartier.' **99**

She says the same to most of us, Sharon

"That's me, international rock star and gravy maker extraordinaire."

Ozzy: man of many talents

"I don't want to go on a boat. You can't take a shit on boats can you? Like aeroplanes and tour buses, you can't shit on them."

Have you tried using the toilets, Kelly?

"I love the smell of armpits in the morning – it's like victory."

Who says Ozzy's bonkers?

"I'll go to the gynaecologist for you Kelly, because I feel like a c***."

Imagine how the gynaecologist would feel, Ozzy

"To be Ozzy Osbourne?
It could be worse.
I could be Sting."
Yeah, but think of all that tantric sex, Ozzy

❝I love you all, I love you more than life itself, but you're all fucking mad.**❞**
Same here, Ozzy. Same here

The best gossip, news, pictures, interviews, star style, horoscopes and a seven-day TV guide – every single week!

heat

the week's hottest celebrity news

Subscribe to heat

Every single Tuesday *heat* brings you the best celebrity quotes, hottest gossip and most revealing celebrity pictures. Add to this the stars' latest style tips, best reviews, amazingly accurate horoscopes and a full seven-day TV guide and what you've got is the complete low-down on all your favourite stars!

Get the latest celebrity news delivered to your front door every single week by subscribing to *heat* for just **£66 for 1 year** (51 issues) and save 10 per cent on the cover price, or pay **£33 for 6 months** (26 issues). Call the *heat* subscription hotline now quoting HE02

Alternatively you can subscribe online by visiting
www.emapmagazines.com

SUBSCRIPTIONS HOTLINE
01858 438884

UK offer only, closing date 01/10/2003